I AM D(

MW00452499

I AM DOING IT FOR YOU

Reginald Dancil

Multidimensional Management
Atlanta, GA

I'm Doing It For You: Journey to Realizing that He Was There All the Time

Copyright 2019 Reginald Dancil

Learn more about the author at
www.Multidimensionalmgt.com

ISBN: 978-1-7336407-0-1 (print)
ISBN: 978-1-7336407-1-8 (ebook)

LCCN: 2019933423

Printed in the United States of America

Edited by Nikita Kanev, Allwrite Communications

Cover image: stained glass window at Trinity Lutheran Church in Faribault, MN

DEDICATION

To the memory of my paternal grandmother, Ms. Almena Dancil.

To my goddaughter, Dr. Stephanie Nicole Smith-Rogers, my godson, Brandon Rogers, and my great godchildren, Austin A. Rogers, Ethan A. Rogers, Ashton A. Smith, Brian Johnson, Carmen Johnson, as well as a host of other godchildren.

Most importantly, this book is dedicated to Jesus Christ, who died so that I, in Him, would have eternal life upon my earthly departure.

CONTENTS

ACKNOWLEDGEMENTS

Perhaps the only regret I have is that I never married and had children. While I might still get married, I have no plans on becoming a father in this lifetime. Despite this, however, I am a surrogate father to many.

To my goddaughter, Dr. Stephanie Nicole Smith Rogers. She melts my heart every time I see her. I am very proud of this young lady, who is also a mother, a friend and the daughter I never had. Her wonderful brother, Brandon, is the son I always wanted. To their children: Austin, Ethan, Ashton and, McKenzie. I will always be your "Papa." Those boys hold a very special place in Uncle Reggie's heart.

To my best friend, Ms. Joyce Ann Armstead Smith. Everyone in the world needs a Joyce. She is not only my best friend, she is my check and balance. Whenever I am on the wrong path, she is there to correct me and set me straight. We are joined by the Spirit of God. I was so honored when she and Archie selected me as the godfather to their children.

Two of the greatest memories of my life happened before my grandsons, Ethan and Ashton, were born. I was attending Brandon's t-ball practice. After the session was over, I said good-bye to the rest of the family and headed for my car. As I walked away, I could sense someone running up behind me. I turned and saw it was Austin. He grabbed my hand and we walked together. I have always been grateful to God for him. The other memory was when Stephanie said to me the best gift she could have for Christmas was me

Stephanie's mother often tells me that I am a sucker for Steph, Brandon and my godchildren. I always reply, "yes, and I am proud of it." There's not a better sucker in the world.

To Cora Johnson. Every child needs a Mrs. Cora in their life. There was a time when I was in high school where everyone wanted a gold tooth. I knew Mama Dancil would not approve, as she always wanted me to be my own person. Mrs. Cora intercepted on my behalf to Mama Dancil, and I got my gold tooth.

To Ashley Lloyd and Tiffany James. You both hold a special place in my heart.

To Charlene Butler Daise, a prayer warrior whom I am honored to know.

To Rebecca Thompson Smith, my Caucasian sister.

To Charlene Engle, my Caucasian sister by another mother. I give you these words of Philippians 1:6, "*And I am sure of this, that he who began a good work in you will bring it to completion at the day of Jesus Christ.*" Whatever God has called you to do, He will find you and help you perform it.

To Jewel Riddle, whom I gave away in marriage and who loves me unconditionally.

To Beverly Bannister, and our wonderful relationship.

To Audrey Battle, who possesses a great mind and soul.

To my Waffle House retiree buddies; James, Charlie, Jesse and Henry King.

To Marshall Roberson, who is not only my mechanic but a man of integrity.

To James Powers, who saw God in me.

To Brendal B Davis, my organizer, my planner and my buddy.

To all the other friends and loved ones in my life who have helped me in some way throughout the decades: you know who you are. I am honored that God ordained that we meet.

To Kirby Clements, who told me during one of our many conversations, *"Reg, I love the Lord."* I echo those sentiments, as I also love God with all my heart, body and soul. I am forever grateful for Kirby, and the power of God manifested through him laying his hands on me.

To Ruben Perry, the business mans' business man

To James "Big Jim" Williams, High School Athletic Director and my role model

Most importantly, this is for God. Here on Earth, I am on assignment for God, and He has created, gifted, and sharpened my skills so that I may go forth to testify for Him and His wonderful son, Jesus. Amen.

Chapter 1

HUMBLE BEGINNINGS

I was born in 1943, only 78 years after slavery was abolished. I was raised in the Sulphur Springs Community in Tampa, Florida. At that time, Ku Klux Klan members lived all around the small community, especially to the north. I grew up with a fear of the northern part of town and was raised to travel through it at my own risk. There was too much of a chance of being harassed by the Klan. Sometimes, I would venture there to play in the fields, which would make up Bush Garden and the University of South Florida in today's world, but I was always afraid.

Anyone experiencing racism can relate to this truth: you can sense hatred in the air. You can even sense it in your soul and spirit. Hatred and its cruel cousin racism are both so powerful that you know when they are in operation. Just like you can sense the power and presence of love, so, too, can you sense racism and hatred.

Growing up, there were several racial boundaries in general I was taught, as an African American, never to cross. Blacks stayed with blacks, and whites stayed with whites. This was a universal law unless a white person hired you. Two of my uncles, Edmon and James, were in the unusual position of being able to mingle outside of the black community, as they owned their own construction and plumbing businesses. They were often contracted to perform in some of the predominantly white communities. Some of the people who employed them lived in communities that were known to be racist. Totally against the interaction of races, even for repair work, they would refer to other white people who hired my uncles, by derogatory names because they had hired African Americans. Even though they were able to integrate through work, my uncles endured their fair share of racism. They paid it no heed and made sure to complete their work as best as they could. They did, however, make sure they were clear of those areas before the sunset.

Another uncle of mine, Uncle Gaines, actually pointed his rifle at a white man who was attempting to enter his yard to sell him insurance. It's amazing that he was not arrested or worse for his actions. But Gaines was never afraid of doing what he felt was right. He would always tell me he was standing against white oppression.

Hernando County was about 40 miles north of Sulphur Springs. During the 1920's, Hernando had one of the highest rates of lynching in the country. That fact was just one of the reasons I was told to be home by nightfall.

It was in this environment, one fraught with tension and segregation, in which I was born.

I was born to John Ira Dancil and Naomi Lorraine Eady/ Hardy on April 6, 1943. My mother became pregnant at a mere 15 years of age, something that came as a shock to everyone, especially my grandparents.

Since my paternal grandparents were both well-educated, having obtained some level of higher education, they expected their son to do the same. It was hard to accept that their son, who was only 17-years-old at the time and preparing for college, had gotten someone pregnant. My maternal grandparents, on the other hand, were not very well educated. My maternal grandfather had only completed school up to the sixth grade, and my maternal grandmother may have gone a little farther. This was due to the fact that, when they were children, education was simply not as important as working the fields.

My father, John Ira Dancil, was the only child of my paternal grandmother. He grew up in a home that was spiritually, intellectually and socially advanced. As a young man, my father sang and played both the piano and trumpet. His mother gave him vocal and piano lessons. This helped him to stand out in school and the business community. I remember him as being about 5'10" with a muscular build. He was always dressed to the nines and very articulate. He was well-educated, handsome and had great social skills. My father was a man who treated everyone with respect and honor, no matter their status or rank in life. He told me he was often called a "smooth operator" as a teenager because so many females were attracted to him.

My mother and father never married, as he went away to college shortly after I was born, and my mother sought other relationships. They continued to stay in contact for my sake. My mother didn't always find nice men to date. I recall a time when we were living on Buffalo Avenue and she was dating a man whom I will refer to as "T." He was a large man, certainly much larger than mom, who smelled of cigarette smoke. He was in the military, so even though he was slender, he was very strong. The problem was his quick temper; he always seemed to be angry about something. There was a night where he and my mother got into a fight, and he beat her so badly that she was bleeding from around the eyes. Unable to take it anymore, I stood up from the sofa and yelled out his name. I hadn't even taken two steps before he whirled around and slapped me so hard that I fell back onto the sofa. Undeterred, he continued beating my mother.

At that time, my father was to marry a woman named Edna Douglas, who was from Newport News, Virginia. Edna was a beautiful, graceful, strong-willed woman. Even though I was not her child, she always showed me kindness. Edna came from an admirable background. Her family, like my father's family, believed in the power of a higher education and raised her with love and affection. They would go on to have three beautiful children.

While living with my mother, I would frequently visit my grandmother. She lived in an apartment about six blocks away.

Whenever I visited Grandma Susie, she would always send me to Hargret's Supermarket, giving me a dime so I could buy her three cigarettes or a can of snuff. The owners of the store knew everyone, including my grandmother, so they didn't mind me shopping for her. Whenever she wasn't around, I would grab her can of snuff and place some of the tobacco under my lips, trying to do it just as she did. It was so strong that, if you accidently inhaled the tobacco, it would momentarily take your breath away. Whenever the cans were empty, I would fill it up with any loose change I could find and bury it outside. I made sure to memorize where I had buried it, so it could be dug up later, for whenever I was short on money.

Grandma Susie was kind, but she was strict. Everything always had to be neat and orderly, from the floors to the pantry, which was always organized and spotless. She was the type of woman who would start to clean up even before everyone was finished eating. She was a big believer in the old adage "spare the rod and spoil the child." I remember one day when I got into trouble with her. She later told me to go to my room and get dressed, as she wanted me to accompany her to town to pay some bills. Excited, I went into the bedroom and took off all my clothes. Suddenly, she appeared with a switch in hand and beat me while reminding me of whatever it was I had done.

Even though she was very strict, I loved my grandmother very much. I loved the way she chewed her peach snuff, holding it in her lower lip as she went about her chores. Whenever she sat on the porch, she would try to spit her snuff out further and further away each time, as though it was a personal contest. She would even spit on the bugs flying nearby, causing them to flee.

My grandmother would take me to her church. As a child, I wasn't interested in the service, though. I always looked forward to the food that was prepared after the service. To this day, I can still remember the food that was prepared by members of the congregation. There was always plenty to go around, usually fried chicken, a roast, smothered pork chops, potato salad, and fluffy white rice. There was also a variety of freshly cooked vegetables to go with the meats, like black-eyed peas, green beans, collard greens, and mustard greens. The dessert table was always full of sweet treasures, such as lemon meringue pie, sweet potato pie, pound cake and—my favorite—banana pudding. I don't remember anyone ever telling us the food was ready; rather, the delicious smells would draw everyone toward the buffet. The aroma was so intoxicating that everyone stopped what they were doing, whether it was playing sports or discussing the service. I would always eat outside while the other church members stood around, eating, laughing and talking inside. After we were done eating, the kids would gather around whatever adult was making ice cream for dessert. It was exciting to watch them churn the ice cream by hand. I think the anticipation made the taste of the ice cream that much sweeter.

I will never forget eating dinner at the church on the night someone had accidently disturbed a skunk. Evidently, some kids had been wandering around in the woods and came upon it. They unknowingly chased it back towards the church, where it darted inside and released its powerful spray. The odor was so strong that it seemed to penetrate the food, causing me to gag whenever I bit into it. The smell lingered long after we left. In fact, I could still smell it during the long ride home.

Chapter 2

THE GOOD LIFE

During the 1920's, the first school for African American children was created in Spring Hill, which included Sulphur Springs. Officially, it was called the Spring Hill Missionary Baptist Church. Unofficially, it was known as the "Brown Derby." After I was sent to live with my paternal grandmother, I attended this school in the fourth grade. The building was marketed as new and large enough to accommodate 100 children and several faculty members, as opposed to a white-only school, which comfortably held around 600 students.

When we arrived to start school, the building looked unfinished. It was unpainted, and there were still holes in the floor from where they hadn't finished installing the flooring. We became accustomed to looking down whenever we walked to class. Otherwise, we might get our feet stuck in a hole. It reminded me of an outhouse – both from the smell and its appearance. We used textbooks that had been donated to us from other schools. The inside covers were always filled with the names of Caucasian children who had owned them before us.

Whenever it rained heavily—which was often in Florida—parts of our community would flood. My grandmother told me that, about ten years before I was born, The Tampa Electric Dam collapsed, causing water to rush in and flood Sulphur Springs. Ever since then, whenever it stormed too badly, the Hillsborough River would always overflow into a section of the community, known as "the bottom." It would flood so much, and so quickly, that the people living there could not leave their homes. For days, people would be unable to attend work or school. The heavy rains did not directly affect my home, but I still enjoyed wading through the water with my classmates. We always collected any tadpoles and crawfish we could find. Occasionally, I would see snakes slithering through the water. They would float into people's homes, scaring the people who were trapped inside.

Our community was very small, and it did not have many industries or other economic opportunities for residents to earn a living. There were people who thrived there, nonetheless. People like Mr. Buster Whitehead, who owned and operated a popular poolroom, and the Richardson family, who were all auto mechanics, did well for themselves. People like Shorty, a white man selling mostly candy from his store, did particularly well. Whenever my friends and I came around, he would guard the candy as though it were Fort Knox.

There was an arcade that was attached to a movie theatre. I could not usually afford to go, but whenever I did, I remember thinking it was the greatest place in the world. I never visited the movie theatre; although African Americans were allowed into the arcade, the movie theater was still off limits. They were, however, allowed into the Greyhound Stadium as long as they were placing bets on racing dogs.

Every morning, as I walked to school, I would never see any adults. When I walked home, the only adults I would see were often winos and gamblers. This was because the majority of the adults would board a bus in the early hours of the morning, long before I woke up, where they traveled at least 15 miles a day to work in fields. One day, they would travel to Ruskin to plant or harvest tomatoes. The next day, it was Plant City to manage the strawberries or cabbage. The next day it was unloading bananas at the dock in Port Tampa, which the locals called "Po' Tampa."

In 1950, when I was around 7-years-old, the school I went to was replaced with Dillard Elementary School. Unlike the old school, Dillard Elementary was beautiful. It had an amazing brick structure and was built on a hill, so there was plenty of outside space. After attending the Brown Derby, I remember seeing Dillard and thinking I had died and gone to heaven. It was like moving from the outhouse to the proverbial White House.

My first memories took place around the time I was 4 or 5 years old, when I lived in an apartment on 22nd Street in Tampa, with my mother and my maternal grandmother, Ms. Susie Hardy. My mom was a very attractive woman with a great personality. She was about 5'7" with a very shapely figure. When she smiled, it would emanate from her beautiful soul and shine across her entire face so that even her eyes sparkled when she smiled. She was always immaculately dressed, always matching her jewelry to whatever outfit she had on. She spoke with a soft voice. She had an outgoing spirit that made her a natural leader, as well as an attitude that made her well-liked by her family and friends. She also had a God-given talent for music. She both sang and played the piano. I was the only child between my mom and dad.

My grandmother was a tall woman, about 5'10", with a naturally slender build and dark skin. I always remember her wearing a dress. In all the years I knew her, she never once wore slacks or pants. She was also a very spiritual woman, the one who first planted the knowledge of God in me. She was an elder in her church, which was called the House of Jacob.

Grandmother worked as a maid for a wealthy Caucasian family living on Davis Islands. The islands are known for their views of downtown Tampa, as well as their lavish, pastel Mediterranean–style buildings dating from the 1920's. Many of the homes were large, stately and well-manicured, constructed of light materials and painted with bright colors to reflect the extremely hot climate. Davis Islands was home to many of Tampa's elite. Many of its residents were doctors, lawyers and politicians. These were the men and women who shaped Tampa's history and future. Growing up, I thought this was how all white people lived. There were no black families living on Davis Islands. When I was younger, I would ride with my grandma to her work, taking in all the breathtaking and beautiful homes. The homes even had air conditioners inside, and most of the residents had swimming pools, even though they lived so close to the bay.

It was here that I first got a taste of what I like to call the "good life." Ever since then, I love fine furniture, well-manicured homes, fine clothing and neighbors with similar views about life.

In hindsight, I was already living the good life. My grandmother maintained a strong partnership with the community. Later on, she would build a daycare and kindergarten to watch over small children on behalf of their parents who were out working in the fields. There were many times that neighbors would come to speak to my grandmother, who was known to be an avid spokeswoman. She would always help articulate the concerns of those who felt they did not have the skills to present themselves appropriately.

During this time, there was a lot of mafia activities occurring. Cubans were being gunned down in the streets. I overheard people saying that there was war over who would control the import dock, and the supplies that were being imported from Cuba and other countries. A lot of the fighting took place on 7th Avenue, more specifically, in a section of the town known as Ybor City. This is where my grandmother had to pass through to get to her job. Ybor City was known for its stores that sold cigars, which were all handmade. You could walk into to a shop, request a personal cigar and watch it being rolled. There was also a cigar factory in Ybor City, and the scent of tobacco hung heavy in the air for miles. It became known as the Cigar Capital of the World. My grandmother witnessed several shootings, sometimes in broad daylight. They were becoming more and more common.

During this time, my mother and I lived with my grandmother, along with my Aunt Betty Jean, Aunt Gwendolyn, and Uncle Jay Lee, who was seldom there, as he was enlisted in the military.

While living in my grandmother's apartment, my Aunt Gwendolyn died of a tumor. Aunt Gwendolyn was dark-skinned and slender, a lot like her mom. She had loved to run and play with me and the other children. This was my first experience with death, and at 6 years of age, I didn't understand the permanence or significance of it. I just kept asking what happened and why everyone was crying.

"Don't worry," my grandmother told me. "She's in a better place now."

Chapter 3

SEPARATED

When I was around 8-years-old, my mother told me that my father was coming to Tampa to visit us. It was the first time I had remembered ever seeing him. As soon as he walked into our home, I remember thinking he was very handsome. He was also a well-dressed, soft-spoken man when he greeted the both of us. They told me I was going to his mother's home in Sulphur Springs while they went to watch a movie.

It was around noon when they dropped me off at Grandma Dancil's house. As a child, I was a bit scared of Grandma Dancil. Although only about five feet tall, she was such a spiritual and virtuous woman that her presence seemed much larger. She was a no-nonsense type of person, but that did not make her cruel. She always made herself available and accessible to those in need. As an entrepreneur who owned and operated the only day care center in the community, she was very well-respected in our community. She was a member of The Order of the Eastern Star. She was also the music director for her home church, the

Emmanuelle Tabernacle, and for another local congregation, New Bethel African Methodist Episcopal Church. She also taught piano and vocal lessons. Because she was so involved in the community, everyone respected her, whether it was the people who worked in the business community or the local wino.

While mom and dad were at the movies, I went and joined the kids in the daycare. I played for several hours, until all the other kids were picked up and piano classes ended. Grandma Dancil and I were alone. I was sure that my mother would be by soon to pick me up, but several more hours passed with no sign of my parents. Grandma Dancil—or Mama Dancil, as I called her—cooked dinner as the sun began to set. Later that evening, Mama Dancil gave me a pair of pajamas and told me it was time to go to bed.

I was confused, but I did as I was told. As I entered the bedroom my grandmother told me to go in, I looked around. It wasn't until I was putting on the pajamas that the truth hit me. My heart sank, and I sat down on the bed in shock. I can still remember the pain I felt, even so many years later. As I got into bed and pulled the covers over me, I still hoped that my mother would come and wake me to take me home. But the night came and went, and I woke up in the same room.

I felt numb over breakfast. Even as the days went by, I always held hope that they would return. Every morning, I looked for them. I watched for my father's car, imagining it pulling into the driveway. Eventually, the truth began to set in. I finally realized my mom was not coming to get me. I felt so alone in that house.

The only other person living there was an old woman whom I did not know and didn't really like. I knew she had something to do with the fact that I was no longer with my mother. I started to blame her for the fact that I lived there. I missed my mother like crazy, and I didn't know how to handle my sadness.

For the next 15 years, I would stay with Mama Dancil. During that time, my mother would periodically come and visit me. Whenever she would visit, it was as if we never parted. We would walk to the store and I was proud to be with her. We would hold hands and I would smile, beaming proudly because my mother was there with me. Whenever I asked her if I could come live with her, she always looked sad and shook her head.

Mama Dancil made sure that I was never alone. But despite her best efforts, whenever my mom left, I would go into a deep state of loneliness. Even when Mama Dancil tried to joke with me, I didn't say anything back. Although she treated me well—honestly, much better than I deserved—I still felt like I was a prisoner in her house.

To foster parents, grandparents, and other guardians, the children often don't know how to show them love. That it because they miss their parents so much, and they don't know how to handle or express their loneliness. No matter how much you might love and care for them, you are not their mother. You can fill their space, but you can't take their place. But don't lose faith; one day, they will learn to love and appreciate you. Don't become weary from their lack of appreciation. Keep your faith and hope alive. They will always long for their mother, as she is the one who is linked to them by blood. But if you continue to recognize their God-given talents and nurture it, you will be rewarded with their gratitude.

I used to not like Mama Dancil at all, and I didn't treat her as respectfully as I should have. But now I realize that she was the best thing that could have ever happened in my life. I had no idea at the time that I was right where I needed to be. My life's purpose has been to sing to others and teach them about the gospel; I began to learn how to do these things under the care of Mama Dancil. I was being nurtured and groomed by this elderly woman to become the man I was supposed to be. I do not think God wanted me to be born out of wedlock. He would have preferred my parents to marry and remain together. However, God used my parents' situation to ultimately fulfill His plan.

The world is full of children who are born out of wedlock every day. Those children wander around feeling hopeless, doing everything in their power to find the truth of who they are and what their purpose is in life. I can personally attest that there are no illegitimates in the heart of God. He knew my plight, just as he knows yours. He helped me find my purpose and identity. He is always working to help us find and fulfill our purpose.

He was there all the time.

Chapter 4

REAFFIRMATION

A few days passed and there was still no sign of my mother. I was still going to school at Dillard Elementary at the time. I would often daydream, gazing out of the window and mostly looking for my mom. I always dreaded going home after school. I hated being there, even though my grandmother treated me well. I simply wanted to be with my mom. I couldn't help but feel like I was being controlled there, or maybe oppressed. Some of this was due to the fact that Mama Dancil was a very strict woman. She did not compromise at all when it came to my studies or chores. In addition to my schoolwork, I had to help her clean the house every day. She was also very adamant that I have good manners with others; this not only meant being respectful, but being punctual, as being late was disrespectful to the person who was waiting on you. She also made me attend church with her every Sunday.

I began to suspect the reason she was so strict with me was because she was trying to eliminate the few mistakes my father had made in having me so young. My father had been an obedient and dutiful son up until he had impregnated my mom at an early age. It seemed that Mama Dancil was determined that I would not make the same mistakes. She screened all phone my calls and interrogating any young ladies who called or stopped by the house.

One day, I was slowly walking back to Mama Dancil's house after school when the local wino spotted me. "That's junior Dancil's boy there!" he called out, stumbling around the street. Those were such comforting words during a time of identity crisis.

During this dark time, I never felt as though my mother had disowned me. After all, I still saw her on a regular basis. Somehow, my anger and sadness over the whole situation became directed at the person whom I saw everyday: my grandmother.

For the next fifteen years, I only spoke to her when I absolutely had to, and there were very seldom days where I truly had fun. I was determined not to like Mama Dancil, mostly due to the fact that she wasn't my mother. But there were other reasons why I found myself distant with her; one day, I happened to overhear her on the phone as she was talking to her friend.

"They say he's my boy's son," she mused. "But he doesn't act anything like him."

It took me a minute to realize she was talking about me. Her words cut through me like a knife. After that, I didn't want anything to do with her. It would be many years until I understood how hard it must have been for Mama Dancil to raise me, especially after having raised my father.

Despite the loneliness and despair that often threatened to

overwhelm me, my feelings about God always remained strong. I didn't blame God for my mother not being there; even back then, I knew God didn't want me to suffer.

Mama Dancil lived in a small community, and everyone seemed to know everyone. Because it was the same community that she raised my father in, many people still remembered him. A side effect of everyone being friendly with one another was that there was no such thing as privacy; everyone knew everything about all the people living in that community. It didn't take long for everyone to learn that I was living with my grandmother. Random people would come up to me and start talking about my father, and their memories of him. Most days, I would walk down the street and the people I passed—whether they were sitting on the bench in front of the lumber yard, playing checkers in front of their homes or leaving the pool hall with half empty bottles in their hands—they would all call out to me.

"That's junior Dancil's boy there!" they always said.

They didn't realize it, but their words helped to remind me of my identity. Even if my mother wasn't there with me in person, he was with me in spirit and memories. His blood flowed through my veins. God uses these people to help reaffirm my identity.

I never felt God had abandoned me, as I had been taught during my early years that He was a constant presence. It is as Hebrews 13:5 tells us, "I will never leave you or forsake you." I held tight onto this scripture during this time, clutching the words close until it became a living, breathing passage for me.

I remember the first time I had a clear conversation with God; it was speaking through a direct line with Him, like I had picked up the telephone and He was on the other end. I was early into my teenage years, maybe around fourteen years of old. The conversation actually came as a result of my disobedience to Mama Dancil. She was the pianist for the New Bethel Methodist AME Church Choir and sometimes had to stay quite late to practice or perform. Whenever she had these late nights, she would always tell me to stay home. She didn't want me going to the park late at night, especially by myself.

So, of course, I didn't listen.

I tried my best to be crafty about it. I would stay close enough to the church that I could see the choir members when they left. I knew Mama Dancil wouldn't leave the church until the lights went out; when they did, I would run the three blocks back home, pretending to have been there the whole night. There were several nights that I would wander too far from the church, and I wouldn't see the lights go out until it was too late. The first time this happened, I had lost track of time while playing football. I could feel my heart in my throat as I sprinted back to the house. I called out to God, pleading with Him to stall Mama Dancil so I could beat her home. I promised I would never leave the house again, that I would be a perfect angel from now on, so long as I didn't get caught. When I entered the silent home, having succeeded in getting there before her, I almost fell to my knees in relief.

My promises were short-lived, as the temptation of the playing outside was just too strong to resist. It only took a week for me to return to the park, and it wasn't long before I missed the lights dimming once again. This time, when I raced towards home in a panic, I tried calling out to God again, but the line was closed and silent. I knew there was no way I could ask God to protect me again, not when I had so recently broken my promise to Him. I had no confidence to speak to Him; why should He believe anything I said to Him now? Nevertheless, I kept praying and asking him for mercy. I asked again for Mama Dancil to be delayed, so that I could make it home before her. But as soon as I reached the front door, it swung open to reveal Mama Dancil. She was holding a paddle in one hand and an expression of righteous anger.

Even though I couldn't appreciate it then, I can see now so clearly that God hadn't turned his back on me. He may have seemed silent to my pleas, but He knew the best thing for me was to get punished. God is all loving, but He is also fair. Every sin carries a punishment, and He knew I had to learn this lesson early on. I would continue to learn it throughout my life, proving that God never once abandoned me.

He was there all the time.

Chapter 5

TALENTS
BESTOWED

Before I lived with Mama Dancil, my mother and I moved around quite a bit. The first house we moved into was on Buffalo Avenue; it was a small house, east of Lake Avenue and approximately three blocks from the old apartment. We called it a "shotgun home" because you could see the back door from the front door. My friend told me the reason it was called a shotgun home because if a man was cheating with another man's wife, the husband would see him running out one door and into the path of his shotgun.

I remember one day when mom left the house, telling me she would return later.

"Don't you bother with that package on the counter," she warned me.

Of course, as soon as she left I went directly to the counter and saw what appeared to be chocolate candy. I quickly gobbled it up, thinking I would simply ask for forgiveness when she got home and take my licks. Back then, a few bites of chocolate was worth getting a spanking. My sister Dorothy and I left the house to head for the park. We hadn't been there very long when my stomach began to gurgle furiously; I realized I had to use the bathroom.

I quickly told Dorothy I had to use the toilet and started to run for our house. She followed me, and we rushed home, dashing through the graveyard so fast that we were dodging and jumping over tombstones. But I wasn't quick enough; halfway home, I felt myself start to use the bathroom. It ran down my legs and into my pants, even filling my shoes. It turns out I hadn't eaten chocolate after all, but laxatives that my mother had bought for herself.

As I walked the rest of the way home in my own filth, I thought to myself, Reggie, just do what your momma say from now on. My mother didn't even bother to whip me when I got home. She figured I had already learned my lesson.

But, of course, I would go on to disobey her again. A few weeks passed, and one day I saw she had left her cigarettes out, along with a box of matches. Just like other children, I thought my mother looked so cool when she smoked, and I sought to emulate her. I stole a cigarette and the box of matches and crawled under my bed to smoke. But when I lit the match, flames suddenly shot upwards and ignited the bottom of my mattress. I started to frantically beat at the burning mattress with my hands until the flames went out. I was very lucky that I was not hurt and that I did not burn the house down. Since it was the bottom of the mattress, my mother never even saw it.

A year went by and my mother moved into another shotgun home, still on Buffalo Avenue but on the other side of Lake Avenue. It was in this house that I first felt the presence of God.

It was on a day like any other, and there was a stillness in the house that made me restless. Suddenly, I heard music coming from outside. With nothing better to do, I decided to go check it out. I got up and headed out the front door, towards the sound of music and voices. I remember feeling very calm, like I had a great peace of mind. I walked across Buffalo Avenue, dodging what little traffic there was as I proceeded toward the music. The sun was setting and it was getting dark. The park lights were the only lights on in the area, and the streets where I began to walk were dark.

It was then that I felt the spirit of God. It was as though I was suddenly encapsulated in this feeling of pure peace. Although it was invisible, I could clearly feel it before me, standing somewhat to my right. It seemed to expand, until it covered the entire side-walk and street. In the distance, I could see bright lights and a great number of people gathered around. They were all looking up and watching those standing on some sort of platform. I walked towards them, still surrounded in this unseen presence. A young man walked past me, heading the opposite way as he left the park.

"Hey, what are they doing over there?" I asked.

"They are having a talent show," he replied.

I paused, looking around to take in the people who were gathering in the park.

"I can sing just as good as they can," I said boldly.

He looked surprised, then impressed by my confidence. He turned towards the people and loudly called out to them, "here's a young boy who wants to sing!"

The man who was moderating the talent show heard him and turned to look at me, calling out to me to join him on the stage. As I moved through the crowd, the people standing around moved to let me pass through. Normally, this kind of experience would terrify me. But I was not frightened that day; it was with great confidence that I walked up the stairs to the stage. Both of my parents loved to sing, and I had inherited the same love from them. Even at that young age, I already knew that I wanted to be a professional vocalist. I was always singing, whenever and wherever I could. I also felt strengthened by this unseen presence, the one I had felt when I left my house. Once on the stage, I saw a bunch of equipment, such as microphones and speakers. A few people stood around, holding instruments and waiting. Several other people stood in a line, waiting to sing. When I reached the top of the stairs, I turned and surveyed the people gathered there.

"What's your name?" the moderator asked me.

"Reginald," I replied.

"Alright, Reginald, what're you going to sing?"

I paused, thinking about it. A song suddenly came to me, as though the name of it had been whispered in my ear. "The Glory of Love by The Five Keys," I said.

It was a song that was etched into my soul, as my mom always sang it to me. It was a very moving song about the trials and tribulations of being in a relationship and the glory that is received from such a union.

The contestants who were gathered on the stage were both men and women, young and old. The moderator explained that he would announce a winner once we had all completed our songs; it would be based on how loudly the audience responded to us. When it was my turn, I looked out and sang as passionately as I could. In the end, I won second prize. The moderator presented me with my prize, which was a loaf of bread. As I walked back home from the park, I could still feel the lingering presence from earlier. I walked home in perfect peace; I wasn't even afraid that my mom would scold me for leaving home. When she returned home that night, I presented her the loaf of bread and told her how I had gotten it. She was pleased with me and praised me for having the courage to perform in front of so many strangers.

I was suddenly hit with the revelation that my mother had always been there for me, not only that, but she would continue to be there for me. She was the love of my life. It reminded me of that awe-inspiring presence I had felt earlier that day, the one that had filled me with such joy. Looking back on it now, I think that was the first time I realized a parent's love is similar to that of God's love, and that, just like my own mother, God had always been there. He was always watching, always helping me along.

. . . .

In hindsight, I now realize several things about my experience in the park. While I received my physical DNA from my parents, I received my spiritual DNA from God Himself. As Genesis 1:27 tells us, "So God created man in His own image; in the image of God He created him; male and female He created them." I also realized that God created and designed me to fulfill His plan. As Colossians 1:16 states, "For by Him all things were created that are in heaven and that are on earth, visible and invisible, whether thrones or dominions or principalities or powers. All things were created through Him and for Him."

God had not only given me the ability to sing, but on that night in the park, he gave me the courage to share my singing with the people present. I would never have been able to ascend that stage without Him. He not only gives us all the gifts we need to achieve our goals in life, He also gives us the courage to see those goals through to the end.

I have gone on to use my voice both for teaching others and singing. As a child, I taught Sunday school classes, spoke at church youth events, and even sang on a local radio program (WTMP). Later on, I would get the chance to sing for Gregory and Juanita Baranco, who are prominent car dealership owners in Atlanta. I have also performed for Dr. John Maupin, the former President of Meharry and Morehouse School of Medicine, as well as for former United States ambassador named Andrew Young. I have performed duets with award-winning television journalist Monica Kauffman and recording artists Jean Carne. I provided pre-entertainment for Miles Jaye Davis, an R&B and jazz singer, jazz violinist, songwriter, and record producer. I was also briefly a backup singer for Grammy Award-winning singer Michael Bolton.

One of my proudest accomplishments comes from performing at the Trumpet Awards, a prestigious event highlighting African American accomplishments and contributions. I was invited to perform by civil rights leader Xernona Clayton, who is the broadcasting executive and founder/president of the Trumpet Awards. The event is held annually and is generally sponsored by Turner Broadcasting System. In 1997, I was invited to sing "The Lord's Prayer" at the event. I sang before such attendees as Malcolm X's wife, Betty Shabazz, who died that year; Anthony Mark Hankins, a clothing designer who apprenticed with Yves Saint Laurent, in Paris; Bob Bailey, an actor who starred in The Heat of the Night; Al and Olympic Gold Metalist Florencce Griffith Joyner, and many other nationally and internationally acclaimed individuals.

All of it began with a simple walk to the park. As Proverbs 18:16 states, "A man's gift makes room for him, and brings him before great men." God knew where my singing in the park would lead. He found me at my mom's house and sent me forth to begin my destiny.

Isaiah 46:10 tells us, "I make known the end from the beginning, from ancient times, what is still to come. I say, 'My purpose will stand, and I will do all that I please.'" God created us all before the beginning of time in order to fulfill His purpose. I know there are many of you reading this book that do not know what your purpose is naturally or spiritually. I am no different than you, and if God can plant the seed of purpose in me, then He has done it in you. All you have to do is be ready to receive His blessings. Be available, open minded and open-hearted. Please do not try and be somebody else because you envy what they have in terms of gifts and talents. You can only walk in one pair of shoes: yours. God made you specifically with a plan in mind. Like Ephesians 3:20 says, "Therefore, let Him in your life for He will bless you beyond all you can ask or imagine."

He was there all the time.

Chapter 6

CALLED TO SING AND TEACH

I believe that God has a purpose for each of us. But there are certain skills, or tools, needed to fulfill our destiny. For example, a person cannot be a vocalist without the ability to sing the note or hear the pitch. I have known so many people who were told that they could sing, but, in reality, couldn't carry a tune.

When I was younger, I remember singing once at a party. A young lady named Gloria had thrown the party. Before I went up to sing, she told me that she was taking voice lessons from Ms. Davis, the same woman who taught me. I congratulated her and went out to sing. After I was finished, Gloria announced that she was going to sing as well. I was shocked when all the guests started yelling out, "No, no!"

"Come on now, don't be rude," I admonished them. "This is Gloria's party. Let the poor girl sing!"

But when Gloria stood up and started her song, I couldn't help but cringe along with everyone else. The girl was worse than bad;

she was completely tone-deaf. About two weeks later, I saw her out and about. She came up to me said, "Mr. Dancil, I am not taking voice lessons from Ms. Davis anymore."

"Why?" I asked.

She sighed and shook her head. "Ms. Davis told me that God blessed everyone with something, but— for me—that something wasn't singing. She told me I was wasting my money on lessons."

While that may sound a bit harsh, there is some truth to what Ms. Davis told her. If you waste your time pursuing talents that were not given to you, you might be neglecting the talents you do have. I don't believe people should ever give up on their dreams, but I also believe it's important to nurture the talents that God did bless you with. It's as Exodus 35:25 tells us, "all the women who were skilled in sewing and spinning prepared blue, purple, and scarlet thread, and fine linen cloth."

As a teenager, I loved to play the piano in my spare time, usually under the watchful eye of Mama Dancil. I spent many nights with Mama Dancil as she played the piano. I would sing along to the music, letting it fill the emptiness inside me. The music helped to ease the pain that came whenever I thought of my mother and how I didn't want to live without her. I remember practicing the piano until my fingers were flying over the keys.

When I was around 14-years-old, I remember sitting before the piano at Mama Dancil's house. She gave lessons to children in our community, and there were a few times she had sat me down and shown me the basics. One day, I ran my hands over the keys and thought about how much I loved playing the piano. I even said it aloud to myself as I traced the keys in wonder. But as soon as the words came out, I saw Ronald appear in the window. Ronald was one of my football buddies. He considered himself a man's man and had told me in the past that singing and playing piano was for girls. He had been walking by my grandmother's house when he saw me sitting at the piano through our front window. When I looked up and saw him standing there, he grinned and whistled at me like I was a girl he liked. After that, I never took another piano lesson. I fell into his way of thinking that only girls played piano. There isn't a day that goes by that I don't regret that decision. God may have granted me with the talent to play piano and, by choosing to neglect that talent, I lost it forever.

.   .   .   .

I used to teach Bible studies for nine years under the leadership of a wonderful pastor named Cornelius Lynn Henderson. Pastor Henderson once told me, "A pastor needs a pastor." He told me I was that person to him, and I admitted he was that person to me. When I first met him in 1977, it was at a Waffle House located in College Park. I had a Salem 100 cigarette behind my left ear and three marijuana joints in my wallet. He was the one who first invited me to attend Ben Hill United Methodist Church, where he was the pastor. This would become the beginning of a great and long-lasting relationship. He always called me his son in Christ, despite the fact that I was only a few years younger than he was.

He would speak often about hearing from God, so I asked him one day what he meant by that.

"How exactly do you hear from God?" I asked.

I expected a long and complicated response. Instead, he simply said, "Keep doing what you are doing."

As time passed, it began to happen to me. God began to speak to me through His word. There were even a few times where He spoke directly to my spirit, but that has been a rarity. God has made it clear, through His voice and His word, that my purpose in life is to minister to the heart and souls of people. He wants me to use my voice to sing and preach His words. Ever since I was a boy, I wanted to sing. God instilled that desire in me from a young age in order for me to fulfill my purpose. And so I have; all of my life, I have used my voice to sing and teach. As Philippians 1:6 tells us, "He who has begun a good work in you will perform it until the day of Jesus Christ." So, I will continue to praise Him until the day Jesus Christ returns.

I remember when I was taking vocal lessons from Ms. Davis. During one such lesson, she said, "Mr. Dancil, if you are singing and the musician drops the music, don't you stop. Just keep on singing and the musicians will find where you are."

Shortly after she said that, it just so happened that she lost her place and the music faltered. Hearing this, I stopped singing. Ms. Davis sternly admonished me, saying, "Didn't you hear what I said? Don't you ever do that again." Even though I was mad at being chastised at the time, I held her words close to my heart. I applied her words not only to singing, but to my life. Even when life got tough, I would tell myself, "don't you dare stop." I will always cherish my experiences with that wonderful woman.

A person cannot be a professional singer without possessing a good voice. Just like this is true, so it is true that there are certain things a person cannot do without first possessing the necessary skills. Therefore, I believe He has equipped us with the appropriate skills or talents to accomplish our goals.

As I mentioned earlier in this book, God revealed His plan and purpose to me as a child. He instilled a love for singing and teaching from childhood, and I have used my voice to teach and to sing ever since. Even as a teenager, I taught Sunday School classes, spoke at youth events held at church and sang on local radio programs. My disposition for teaching was so obvious at an early age that I was voted "Substitute for the Teacher" while I was in high school.

Looking back on my life, it seems so obvious now that teaching and singing is what I was meant to do with my life. It was why God created me; it's why he established that love for singing in my heart and soul at such a young age. He planted the seed of ministry in my family, who then passed it onto me. I can only hope my voice has helped to pass along the Word of God to others.

HABITUAL LIAR

G rowing up with Mama Dancil was not always easy. As I've said before, she was a very strict woman with rigid morals. At some point, I started to rebel from these morals. It began small.

I would tell a little white lie just to see if she could tell. Then it graduated to stealing from my grandmother's gleaner, which was a paper booklet that was being used by women's organizations. They were used to collect dimes for special occasions.

Mama Dancil was a clever woman, so I did not get away with many crimes. But that didn't stop me from trying. She started to catch me in so many lies that she eventually told me I was a habitual liar. Sometimes, I would lie to her even when the situation did not require a comment or reply.

There were a few days where I was told I could go home early from church, but I wasn't allowed to watch television. Every time I went home, I would turn on the T.V. When Mama Dancil arrived home, she would ask me if I had obeyed her.

"Of course," I replied.

"You're lying," she would respond flatly.

I always denied it, but she seemed to know the truth. No matter how early I turned the television off, she would know if I had watched it. One day, I came home early but did not turn on the T.V. When Mama Dancil came home, I remained silent, so she would think I was gone. I stayed hidden in the hallway and watched as she entered the house. As she passed by the T.V., she ran her hands gently over the screen. I realized she was checking for any static electricity that would have been created from me turning on the T.V.

Lying started to become like second nature to me, until I was speaking more in lies than truth.

I believe it was William Shakespeare that said, "Oh, what a tangled web we weave/ when we practice to deceive." It was true that I was becoming a habitual liar; I was weaving such a complex web of lies every time I opened my mouth. Lying, like anything else, becomes much easier to resort to the more you do it. My first inclination was to tell a lie, or to stretch the truth. But my problem was this: I wasn't a very good liar. I would often trip myself up by telling a different lie than one I had previously told, thereby convicting myself. I was always getting caught. I just couldn't keep up with everything that I told people.

When I was around 16-years-old, Mama Dancil mentioned her friend, known as Ms. Florence. Immediately, I interjected and said I had spoken to Ms. Florence that day. Not only that, but Ms. Florence had told me to say hello to Mama Dancil for her.

"You saw Florence today?" Mama Dancil asked, her eyes narrowed. The way she said it made it sound more like a statement and less like a question.

"Yes, ma'am," I replied, nodding. Then I went off to my room, thinking nothing else about it.

Later that evening, Mama Dancil called me into the living room. She was standing next to the potted plant that I had just bought her for Easter. She had a steely look in her eye as I walked in and stood in front of her.

"I just got off the phone with Florence," she said.

My heart began to race in my chest. I tried to keep my face expressionless, but I could feel the blood leaving my head.

"Florence said she did not see you today," Mama Dancil continued, her voice low. "Tell me, who is lying? You or Florence?"

I hesitated, thinking about how to answer. Mama Dancil obviously knew the truth... and yet, I still stood there in silence and tried to think of another lie I could say to get myself out of the one I had already told. Mama Dancil must have sensed the truth behind my hesitation, because the next thing I knew she had grabbed the potted plant and flung it against the wall. I can still remember feeling the air on my cheek as it whizzed past.

Despite her frustrations with me, and despite our fights, Mama Dancil didn't give up on me. There were still many nights that she would play the piano into the late hours of the night; I would be beside her on the bench, singing along. Sometimes, while I was singing, I would get so carried away in the music that my arms would raise up. Because of Mama Dancil's training, I was able to sing on a local radio show. Not only did she teach me how to sing, she also helped me improve my spelling; When I was around 12-years-old, I entered a spelling bee contest and placed second. There were many, many more accomplishments that I was able to achieve, only because of the love that woman showed me.

A caretaker's love for a child is similar to that of God, in that they love unconditionally. I was not Mama Dancil's son; she could easily have kicked me out of her home at any time, especially when I started lying to her face. But she continued to work with me and teach me the lessons I needed to become a good man. She was there all the time for me, just like God is there all the time. He, too, loves us unconditionally, even when we sin and spit on His image with our deceits.

It is like Psalm 86:15 tells us, "But you, O Lord, are a God merciful and gracious, slow to anger and abounding in steadfast love and faithfulness." Even though I wasn't always respectful to Mama Dancil—such as when I lied to her—she never turned her back on me. She truly had God's love working through her, even when I resisted that love.

He was there all the time.

Chapter 8

ENCOURAGED

I was blessed with great athletic skills. I played several sports throughout my childhood, but I was especially drawn to football, baseball and track. Despite my athleticism, however, there were several times throughout my life where I came close to drowning; one such incident occurred when I was playing "Horse" at Summer Camp. "Horse" is a game we used to play whenever swimming in which we tried to dunk each other's heads under water. My friends and I got so competitive that some of us came close to drowning. We made sure to play it whenever there weren't any adults around, as we knew they would not approve.

When I was attending Dillard Elementary School, there was a teacher there named Ms. Mable Walker. Dillard Elementary was located about 5 miles away from a lake, and Ms. Walker was married into the family that the lake was named after. She was the first woman I remember having a crush on. She was an unbelievably beautiful woman. Not only was she attractive, she was also incredibly charming and kind. I remember an incident where I was tracking a fly ball down and I ran straight into a tree. The pain was intense; I knew right away that there would be bruises under my chin. When Ms. Walker saw what had happened, she rushed over and sat with me, blowing on the bruises until the pain was replaced with a feeling of heavenly bliss. I thought about running into the tree again just so I could receive more attention from her.

While preparing for the trip to Walker's Lake, I went to a local department store with a few of my buddies. As I watched them looking around and trying on swimming trunks, I couldn't help but feel bitter towards them. I didn't have any money of my own, as I was too young to have a job and Mama Dancil didn't believe in giving out handouts. I saw a pair of swim shorts that I loved; they were long and red, which is my favorite color, and had blue and yellow flowers all over them. I fingered the material, marveling at the deep pockets on each side. I contemplated stealing them, but I hesitated. I remembered something Mama Dancil had told me once, after she had caught my stealing a few dollars from her purse. She had told me she was afraid of me.

"What do you mean?" I asked her.

"If you steal, then you will lie. If you lie, then you will kill. So, I am afraid of you."

I was blown away by her words. They were so impactful to me that I carried them with me all throughout my life. Those words stopped me from stealing those shorts. They were so powerful that I still hold onto them today, over sixty years later.

Later that day, my classmates and I rode down to Walker's Lake. The children rode the county bus while our chaperones travelled in their own vehicles. We headed away from the city, leaving the paved streets behind and entering the long dirt road that led to the property. Upon arriving at the lake, I saw the most beautiful cherry trees. Each tree was bursting with bright red and delicious cherries.

It was a hot day in Tampa, and there was not a cloud in sight. The lake was clean and clear,but there were signs posted around the shore warning swimmers to avoid certain areas. Most of the kids were so excited to finally arrive that we immediately headed for the lake. The lake was so large that many people brought their boats there, fishing out on the water for hours. It seemed easier to breathe there. The air was pristine since there were no factories and big buildings around. My friends and I liked to collect rocks from the edge of the lake and throw them out over the water, trying to see who could skim them furthest across the surface.

My friends and I leapt into the lake, venturing out until our feet barely scraped the bottom. Suddenly, my foot slid into a deep drop-off and I began to sink. I remember seeing the surface getting further and further away, and I swear that my life flashed before my eyes. I knew that if I began to panic I would drown. It wasn't long before my feet touched the bottom of the lake. I steeled myself and pushed off the slippery surface, frantically pumping my legs and swimming up towards safety. As I swam to the shore, I couldn't help but think of the swim shorts I had almost stolen, with its deep pockets; if I had been wearing them, I surely would have drowned.

.   .   .   .

Even as a youth in elementary school, I had great reverence and respect for the Word of God. One scripture that always stuck with me was Jeremiah 7:23, which states that obedience is better than sacrifice. It is paramount to be obedient to God's will. Failure to do so always results in unhappiness and despair, for that person went against what was best for them. I've always strived to have a personal relationship with God; I sensed that if I was without His protection, I would not make it back safely through life.

In that moment at the lake, when I was underwater and feared I would drown, there was an instance when my life flashed before my eyes. I saw an image of me drowning, unable to go back up to the surface. I started to panic, but then the image of me drowning was surrounded by a powerful presence. Suddenly, I saw myself ascending. I felt something lifting me up, encouraging me to head back for the shore. My feet hit the bottom of the lake and I pushed against it with a strength I did not possess on my own. It was only with God's intervention that I was able to make it back to safety.

Just like I ventured too far from the surface and into the lake, so did I venture away from the Lord throughout my life. But no matter how much I strayed from the surface, God was always there to guide me back to the shore.

He was there all the time.

Chapter 9

OPEN RACISM

I'm one of the few people lucky enough to say I've always had employment; from the time I started working at 14 years of age, I went through a variety of careers. I first worked as a paperboy before becoming a trusted worker at Joe's Market, which was a local store that sold mostly fruits and vegetables. I even did a brief stint helping my brother, Lawrence. We were both hired on as plumbers for a company that was owned by our uncle.

After that, I was hired on at Mave's Five and Dime Department Store. It sold a variety of household items, including jewelry, clothing, hardware, and even had dining room furniture. I was on the way to work my shift one day, having taken the county bus directly from school to work. As I departed the bus, I saw a policeman standing next to a man wearing a suit. The policeman saw me coming off the bus and turned to the suited man.

"I guess it's going to rain today," said the policeman.

"Why?" asked the other man, looking confused.

The policeman cut his eyes towards me again. "Because a dark cloud just passed by."

I pretended not to hear their conversation. When the traffic light changed, I quickly crossed the street and hurried into work. When my boss asked me how my day was going, I said it was fine. I didn't speak to him—or anyone else—about what I had heard. It was too hard back then to tell who was racist and who was not.

There were two grocery stores in our community whose proprietors were openly racist. Whenever my family purchased items from them—whether it was meat, cheese or fruits—they always picked out the oldest food to give us. They did not even care if you watched them set aside the freshest food and give you the rest. As far as they were concerned, if we were upset then we could shop elsewhere.

After school, I would head to Mave's to clean out the trashcans, sweep the floors, clean the windows and bathrooms. The owner took a liking to me. On the weekends, I would go to his house and pick up the trash around his property or clean the boat he had docked in the Hillsborough River.

My boss wasn't the only one who took a liking to me. Shortly after I started working at the store, there was a girl who would come in and always seek me out. She was beautiful with pale skin and hazel eyes. It seemed like every day I worked, she would show up unannounced. I knew she liked me from the way she stared at me with those hazel eyes, never looking away.

I was at my boss's house one weekend, cleaning his front porch, when I saw the girl emerge from the house across the street. She stared when she saw me, gazing like she did when I was working.

48

Neither of us waved, however. We simply made eye contact before I turned away and went back to work.

It was apparent to everyone else at the store that she liked me. The other store clerks started to tease me about it, joking that she was following me. These words made me nervous. This was about the time that Emmitt Till— a 15-year-old black child—had been brutally killed in Money, Mississippi. While interracial relationships were happening all over Tampa, they were generally kept a secret. As much as I loved receiving the attention of such a beautiful girl, I started to dread the sight of her. I could feel my co-workers keeping their eyes on me. They knew she wanted to get to me, and they were wondering what I would do.

It was a small town, and it wasn't hard for gossip to spread like wildfire. If anyone started to spread rumors about us, I knew it wouldn't be long before her family heard them. The last thing I wanted was for them to think I was sexually assaulting their daughter, so I made sure to stay far away from her. It was one of the hardest things I had to do, for I was only 15 and had a love for the ladies. But whenever I was about to give in and talk to her, I felt a presence inside me. It would speak to me, telling me to stop and stay away. God knew my heart, and He wouldn't let me fall. He knew His plans for me would be realized, even if I did not.

. . . . .

Growing up, my friends and I always knew to be home before dark.

Whether my family gathered for a picnic, party or reunion, we always made sure to leave well before nightfall. If you were caught out after dark, it was almost a guarantee you would be heckled, or worse. I learned this lesson the hard way; one night, a car chased me home. Two white males were attempting to either scare me or run me over.

I'm sure there were other incidents of racism directed at me, but I was fortunate enough to be shielded from the worst of it by the adults in the community. The adults knew how to work the system; often times, they held key positions in Tampa, and wielded this to their advantage.

The elders of our church also protected us. They strived to give us guidance and help us forgive those who taunted us. Many of the elders were prominent businessmen in our community, so they weren't afraid to stand up to others, even to the police. I learned so much from them, especially on the importance of standing up for myself.

As I look back on my childhood, I can see that many of the men in our community worked for Caucasians, but they did not bow down to them. They were men of great character, and many times their strength was in the form of silence and endurance. I had my family, friends and members in our community to teach me that we are all the same, despite our upbringing or the color of our skin.

While I was still attending college, my father was able to get me a summer job in Washington D.C. He was an officer with the Washington D.C. Metropolitan Police Department; he also owned several businesses throughout the city. My father and I had slowly rebuilt our relationship over the years, talking more and more. I was a little nervous about how his wife would treat me, as she was not my mother. I shouldn't have worried; Edna always treated me as though she had given birth to me. She was the type of woman who said what she meant and meant what she said. I will always be indebted to her kindness and genuine love. During this time, my father and I grew even closer. I was very proud of him for everything he had accomplished.

During the summer I was employed in Washington, D.C., the company I worked for would organize events for at-risk children. That summer, we took the children to a summer camp in Prince Frederick County, Maryland. The week we went to the camp, the counselors would take the children on walks around the area. The children were never allowed to walk alone. On several occasions, we had to hurry the kids back towards the camp, as Caucasian men would try to chase or hit us.

A few years later, my buddy Sam told me he was planning on driving from Tampa to San Bernardino, California, to start a new life on the West Coast. He had a sister who lived there, and he was planning on staying with her for the time being. Since I no longer had a job, I decided to join him. We stopped in Biloxi, Mississippi, to refuel the car and grab some refreshments. Inside the gas station, there were several drink machines behind the counter.

The lady behind the counter was a large, white woman with straw-colored hair. When I walked in, she stopped what she was doing and narrowed her eyes at me.

"Can I help you?" she called out.

"I would like a drink," I responded, approaching the counter. "Strawberry, please."

"We're out of strawberry," she said.

I looked behind her and saw the strawberry machine was still running, but I said nothing.

"Then I'll take orange," I said.

"We don't have orange," she said.

"What do you have?" I asked, starting to feel frustrated.

"We ain't got nothing," she said shortly. We stared at each other for a few moments with the sound of the drink machines whirring behind her. Then Sam and I turned and left the store.

I learned early in life that hatred is more grievous to the person who is hating than the one who is hated. Even though racism was a constant throughout my life, I've tried to never take it personally. Although there were many times in my life where I could have been harmed, I was always protected by God's grace. He was always there with me, making sure I didn't come into harm's way.

He was there all the time.

Chapter 10

STAY AND ENDURE

Afuter I graduated from high school in 1961, I moved to St. Petersburg, Florida, to attend Gibbs Junior College. After I graduated from Gibbs with an associate's degree, I was accepted into Bethune-Cookman College in Daytona Beach.

In my first year there, I learned how much harder it would be than Gibbs. Up until this point, I made decent grades without having to do much studying. Because I had not developed good studying habits, Bethune-Cookman was a rude awakening for me. I was only able to maintain average grades, generally C's. It wasn't until I took a statistics and analysis class that my attitude began to change.

Dr. Byung H. Nam was the professor of the class; he was a man of about 5'7" with a muscular build. Whenever he spoke, it was always soft-spoken, but direct. He treated everyone with patience and respect. On the first day of class, Dr. Nam stood in front of the class and predicted that—statistically speaking—no one in the class would make an A. He said the highest grade achieved would be a low B, with the majority of us getting a C or lower.

If you haven't realized from my experiences with Mama Dancil, I wasn't the kind of man who took kindly to others telling me what to do. I decided then and there I was going to make an A and prove the professor wrong, no matter what it took. I moved up from the middle of the classroom to the front row, taking meticulous notes. I studied late into the night. In the end, I received a low A in the class; but it was still an A.

My college advisors encouraged me to enroll in extracurricular activities in order to stand out amongst the other students. After much deliberation, I decided to pledge to a social fraternity called the Cavaliers and Cavalettes. A social fraternity is a general group that aims to build character qualities in its members, such as leadership and loyalty. I also joined several sports teams. Track became one of my favorite pastimes. I specialized in sprinting, specifically the 100-yard-dash. Several of my track buddies went on to have professional careers, such as Jerry Simmons, who signed on with the Atlanta Falcons as a wide receiver. Another one of my classmates was Larry Little, who would later go on to join the Pro Football Hall of Fame while playing with the Miami Dolphins. Larry was a great guy, with a pleasant personality. He was always very gentle and quiet until it came time to play football.

While I was trying to decide on what clubs to join, I couldn't help but remember all the nights that I spent singing with Mama Dancil. I decided to join the Choir was at Gibbs Junior college.

One year, our choir was invited to perform at several churches in Washington D.C. I called up my father to tell him we were coming to D.C., and he and his wife, Edna, decided to throw us a party. They were the perfect hosts, serving us dinner and being attentive to any needs we may have had. Needless to say, the other members of the choir were impressed. My family and I were the talk of the tour.

After I graduated from Gibbs Junior College in 1963, I decided I wanted to continue my education. Although there were several schools that accepted me, I ended up narrowing down my favorites to Florida A & M University, otherwise known as FAMU, and Bethune-Cookman College.

The deciding factor came when I traveled to FAMU. While walking around the campus, I saw some of my classmates from high school and junior college. In high school, they had been the playboys, drinkers and smokers. Judging from the way they were already acting, I knew that I was not going to go down a good road with them around.

After I returned home, I pondered which way to go. Although it was tempting to attend FAMU with my friends, I knew I would likely end up in trouble there. In my heart, I knew I had to go somewhere else. I thought of Mama Dancil, and all the hard work she had put in, just so I could get a college education. Ultimately, I decided to enroll at Bethune-Cookman College.

During the time between graduating from Gibbs and starting at Bethune-Cookman, I worked at a department store located on

Florida Avenue, about four blocks from Mama Dancil's house. I would often complain to my boss, Mr. Klein, about Mama Dancil, whom I referred to as a tyrant of a grandmother. I was around 19-years-old, and I thought I was grown. I wanted to be on my own and experience life outside of her four walls.

Mr. Klein was always a gentleman to everyone he met, and he was also very soft spoken. I never once heard him raise his voice to make a point. No matter how many times I ranted about the same things, he always took the time to truly listen to me. One day, after a particularly long rant about my grandmother, I asked him if I should leave. He offered me these words:

"Stay and endure," he said wisely. "Because you won't always be there."

But Mama Dancil would continue to stay by my side, when she probably shouldn't have. She was filled with God's love, and so she tried to emulate His teachings. In turn, God was always there, working through my grandmother to turn me away from temptation and protect me from evil.

He was there all the time.

Chapter 11

DISRESPECTFUL

During this time, my relationship with Mama Dancil, which had always been fraught with issues, began to grow strained. She would claim repeatedly that I was ungrateful.

"I went without shoes. I went without dresses!" she would scream at me. "I went without so much—all just to send you to college!"

One day, I had enough. When she screamed at me for being ungrateful, I snapped back at her. "You don't have to take care of me," I yelled back. "I can take care of myself!"

My pride had been pricked. I was convinced I didn't need her help anymore, especially when it meant she could throw it back in my face afterwards.

This was by no means the first time Mama Dancil and I had fought like this. In the time after I graduated from Gibbs and before I started Bethune-Cookman, she and I argued all the time. One day, after she had screamed at me, I woke up early and went out to find a job. I ended up getting hired to dig ditches. I was so full of anger and pride that it reflected in my work. I was shoveling at twice the speed as those around me.

"Hey man," one of the veteran diggers, a big man named Lamont, said to me one day, "You're gonna break your back."

"You're just mad because I'm gonna be your boss one day," I joked, wiping the sweat from my forehead.

But it wasn't long before my back did start to ache. The time I spent digging was under the hot sun, and I soon grew dizzy and tired. After ten hours of straight digging, my pride finally began to crack. I dragged my aching body home and stood before Mama Dancil. "I'm sorry for talking to you the way I did," I said to her softly. "I can't dig ditches the rest of my life."

"Are you going to do what I say?" she asked.

"Yes ma'am," I replied. "I will do whatever you say."

Upon graduation from Bethune-Cookman College, I got an apartment and was proud of myself for taking the first step into adulthood, but I was also fearful of Mama Dancil's reaction. I would visit the apartment several times throughout the week just to stand in the rooms and breathe in the air, imagining how it would feel to live there. Whenever I slept, I would dream about it. In my dreams, I was always walking to the front door, but the closer I got to it, the further the door became. I could never touch it, even in my dreams.

I began to feel tormented; I wanted to be truthful with her, but I felt like I could not tell her for fear of what she would say. I even called my father and told him that I wanted to move out.

"I am surprised you haven't moved out yet," he said simply.

"I know it's your mom and I just don't want to cause any problems. I need to tell her I want to leave. But I don't know how to talk to her," I hesitated. "Will you call her and try to talk to her for me?"

"That's fine, I will," he replied.

By this point, I had nearly completed my first year as a teacher. The day after I spoke to my father, I returned home to find Mama Dancil waiting for me at the front door. She greeted me with a smile and asked how my day had been. She didn't seem upset or angry with me at all.

I guess he didn't call, I thought to myself.

Unbeknownst to me, Mama Dancil had been thinking about buying a car for me. It wasn't until I came home the next day that she confronted me, telling me that she had spoken to my dad.

"Really?" I asked, not sure how to respond. She must have known that I spoke with my dad, but I couldn't help playing innocent. Old habits die hard, I guess.

"He told me you wanted to move," she went on.

"Yes, ma'am," I said slowly.

She crossed her arms and looked away.

"I was going to buy you a car," she said suddenly. "I know how you've been needing to get around."

A sudden image came to my mind; it was a picture of me driving Mama Dancil around town, taking her to church and the grocery store every time she needed to go. I would never be able to say no to giving her rides if she was the reason I bought a car. I could feel my independence slipping away from me. I thought of my apartment, empty and waiting for me to move in. I opened my mouth to tell her about it, but nothing would come out. I was still too terrified to tell her.

I realized then how much Mama Dancil controlled me. It may not have been her intent, but she controlled me; she controlled my mind and subsequent actions. I was afraid to leave her home, which my mind was beginning to associate with a prison.

Then it just came spilling out; I told her that I was leaving. I told her about the apartment, and how I had been slowly organizing and packing up my things for the past few weeks, so that I would be ready at a moment's notice. I retreated to my room before she could react, calling a co-worker to pick me up. I quickly moved my meager belongings to the front porch and waited with bated breath. But Mama Dancil did not take the news laying down; when my friend finally showed up, she ran out and chased him away. Then she turned to me with fury in her eyes.

"You are not taking anything I have bought!" she screamed, reaching for my things to take them back inside. I quickly grabbed as much as I could carry and ran off, heading for the nearest payphone. I placed a call to a taxi; true to form, Mama Dancil tried to chase him off as well.

"What the hell, lady!" he yelled as Mama Dancil rushed the car.

"You're not takin' my stuff!" she said again. Frustrated, I grabbed her hands with my own.

"Just let me go!" I shouted.

She looked startled for a moment. Then her face crumpled, and she began to cry, her shoulders shaking with her sobs. I started to reach for her.

"Just go," she said, shaking my hand off.

So, I did. I knew that I had hurt Mama Dancil. I may have even destroyed our relationship. Still, I couldn't help but to be excited as the taxi cab left her behind. I was able to finally move into my apartment. For the first time, I felt like I had been blessed with a sense of greater responsibility and accountability. I bought my first car, which was an early 1960's Bel Air Chevrolet. I didn't know anything about cars, and the guy selling it sensed that. He told me the car didn't have anything wrong with it, and I took his word for it. I had it for a week before it smoked like a chimney. The valves began to rattle, and smoke poured out from under the hood. Having spent all my money, I had no choice but to continue to drive it around. I would often get a headache from all the carbon monoxide the car was emitting.

I'm ashamed to say I did not call or visit Mama Dancil for a couple of years. I felt like I was free from bondage. But as more time went on, I started to realize I was not free at all. Here I was, 24-years-old, and finally living on my own; but while I may have been physically out of Mama Dancil's house, I was still there in spirit. I started to have recurring nightmares where I was still living in her home and afraid to tell her I had an apartment, even though I had moved out weeks ago. It felt like Mama Dancil had cast some kind of spell over me; I couldn't seem to shake her off, no matter what I did.

I am currently 74-years-old and, although I was able to forgive Mama Dancil through the help of Jesus Christ, occasionally I will still have that same recurring dream; I dream I am living in her house again. Every time I try to open my mouth to tell her I'm leaving, the words run dry.

Chapter 12

ACCUSATIONS

I was fortunate to find a job right after I graduated. My neighbor, Raiford B. Allen, was the principal at Booker T. Washington Junior High School, which was the school I had attended as a student. Unbeknownst to me, I was taking the place of another male that Mr. Allen had previously hired. He had been terminated after he'd gotten a student pregnant. I didn't realize it at the time, but everyone at the school was watching me like a hawk.

I made sure to remain professional and not get personal with any of the students. Despite this, one of the students, a girl named Barbara, managed to find my grandmother's phone number from the phone book. She called my grandmother's house in the middle of the night, hoping to speak with me, and I unknowingly answered the phone. The girl had barely spoken a few words when her mother picked up the other line and tried to accuse me of being intimate with her daughter. I attempted to calm the woman down and explain to her that her daughter probably harbored a crush on me, much like I had with Ms. Mable Walker when I was a boy. But the mother refused to listen; she insisted I was up to no good and threatened to go to the police.

Not knowing what else to do, I called Mr. Allen and explained to him the situation.

"I think I'm being set up," I said, desperately.

Mr. Allen assured me that he believed me, and I started to calm down.

"We will still need to have a meeting with the girl's mother," said Mr. Allen. "We want to get this whole thing settled and put behind us as soon as possible."

I agreed with him, convinced that the mother would see reason. On the day of the meeting, I waited with Mr. Allen and his receptionist, Ms. Audrey Spotford. She had been a receptionist there for years, and this was not the first time she had seen a young male teacher get accused for something like this. She was a very kind lady; she had gone to high school with my father, and still remained close to him even in adulthood. I must have looked nervous because she leaned in and patted my hand with hers.

"Don't worry," she said softly. "No one believes that you did anything wrong. This woman is clearly trying to set you up."

I smiled gratefully at her, feeling a bit better, until the girl's mother walked in. She immediately started to glare at me, and I fought the urge to look away and sink into my chair. I finally understood the adage, "if looks could kill". From the way she was eyeing me, I would have been shredded to pieces long ago.

You didn't do anything wrong, I reminded myself sternly.

Still, these were dangerous accusations she was leveling against me. I was all too aware I could lose everything I had worked for, from my job to my small apartment, all from a few words uttered by one woman. I explained to everyone what had happened, but she was not convinced. She continued to accuse me of having some sort of relationship with her daughter. However, she had no proof to back up her words, so the matter was dropped. I taught for eight more months and never heard anything else about the matter.

This was not the first time a female student would try to flirt with me. There was a young girl, around 14-years-old, whom I will refer to as Cheryl. One day, she came up to my desk after class and confessed her love for me.

"I'm going to m-marry you one day, Mr. Dancil," she stammered.

"Cheryl, listen to me carefully," I said, looking her in the eye. "Remain a young lady for as long as you can. But when you do grow up, you will meet the man of your dreams."

She said she understood, but the memory of Barbara still haunted me. After Cheryl left, I immediately went and tracked down her homeroom teacher Ms. Reed. I told her of the situation and asked her to keep an eye on Cheryl.

"If she looks like she's coming to my classroom, please follow her," I begged. I wanted to make sure there was someone else around to witness all my actions so that there would be nothing to use against me later. As a teacher, that was a very difficult time for me. I always felt eyes on me, and it seemed like they were coming from all the students and the teachers combined.

It wasn't just the female students I had to watch out for. Standing at 5'6, I was not a very tall or intimidating man. This caused the male students to think I was a pushover. They weren't the only ones testing me; the male students that had recently graduated from junior to senior high would always come back to campus and get into trouble. It was always the boys who had been a big deal in junior high, the ones who wished for the opportunity to rule over the school once again. I was constantly chasing them away from campus.

It took time, but eventually I was able to win the current students over. I made a strong statement to bullies that they were not going to sneak onto our campus without permission. I always managed to intercept them at the back entrance of the school. These kids were mostly from the projects, and I had no doubt they carried drugs and alcohol to sell to the children inside the school. No matter how much they tried to cajole me, I wouldn't let them pass. There were times we got into heated arguments, and they would curse at me before leaving.

I knew it was important that I didn't cave in to the teenagers. Not only would they try to sell drugs to the younger children, but the kids I taught were always watching me to see how I would handle them. If I showed weakness to the kids who had graduated, I would have lost the respect of the children that were in my class.

I was constantly being tested by my students. One day, a girl by the name of Maxine climbed onto my desk. Maxine was a teenager, but she had the mentality of someone much older. This was due to her upbringing; she grew up in the projects and was constantly dating men older than her. I would often hear her bragging about them to her friends.

Once on my desk, she crossed her legs and said, "Mr. Dancil, I don't have to do any work if I don't want to, do I?"

"Get back in your seat before I call the guidance counselor," I replied sternly.

She slowly got up and returned to her seat. Out of the corner of my eye, I saw a group of boys turn away. They had been watching me to see how I would handle the situation.

While working at the school, I often told the students to always strive for the best in life. It wasn't until my second year there that a thought suddenly seized me, shaking me to the core. It seemed to come from a different place than myself, like a voice was speaking to me.

You're always telling others to strive for the best in life, the voice said. But what about you?

In hindsight, I realize those words came from God. Just like He led Abraham away from his family and to another land, God took me from that position to a place where I would be much happier. Sometimes, we must leave what we are comfortable with to find something better. As Genesis 12:1-3 tells us, "The Lord had said to Abram, "Go from your country, your people and your father's household to the land I will show you.

The next day, I decided to drive to the courthouse and take the federal entrance examination, which was an application for employment with the federal government. I craved the stability that came with working a government job. It was something I had been thinking about for a long time but had never gotten around to doing anything about it.

I passed the entrance examination with flying colors.

After that, I taught for another year before school integration began.

In 1964, the Civil Rights Act was passed, which prohibited racial segregation in schools. Segregation is the systematic separation of people into ethnic groups, generally based on their race. Up until that point, schools had been strictly segregated; Caucasians went to one school and African Americans went to another. There were even separate public bathrooms and water fountains for the different races. After the Civil Rights Act came into effect, public schools began to integrate their students.

Integration was a new concept for the teachers, as well as the students. All my early education was done in segregated schools. Although it was for a good cause, integration caused several problems, one of which was the number of teachers. As the schools began to merge and the students were combined into the same classes, there was a surplus of teachers. The schools couldn't afford to keep paying everyone, so they started laying off teachers. Because I was one of the last people who had been hired at my school, I was one of the first who was let go.

My employment grew sporadic after that. Unable to find another teaching job, I managed to find work at fast food restaurant as a janitor. My pride stung at the thought of making minimum wage, but I had no choice.

I was no longer earning enough money to make my car payment. My debt was slowly smothering me. It wasn't long before I was so broke that I could not afford to drive to work. My gas tank was always verging on empty. During those days, whenever I had to drive up a hill, I would take my foot off the gas pedal and sit up near the steering wheel, letting the car roll downhill in an attempt to save gas.

There were a few occasions where a friend would buy me lunch, for which I was always grateful. Things got so bad that I remember waking up one day and finding only two ends of bread in my refrigerator. I ransacked the cabinets and managed to find peanut butter and jelly, although there was only enough to moisten the bread. That was a low day for me, for after eating, I still felt so hungry. I remember walking out the front door of my apartment, looking around at my neighbors' windows and wandering what food they had in their pantries. At least they don't know I only have peanut butter and jelly, I thought bitterly. For all they know, I might have just eaten a steak dinner.

It was pride—once again—that kept me from reaching out to the multitude of people who would have helped me. Pride filled me even when food could not.

I became so desperate for work that I began to apply every-where. I applied to so many places that I couldn't even remember all the places I went to each day. Eventually, I received a call from Honeywell Aero Space Division in Pinellas Park, Florida, and I began work there later that summer.

The year was 1968, and I was hired on as a Quality Control Specialist. I was responsible for tracking the parts we manufac-tured; these parts would later go on to be used in the NASA's Space Program.

I hadn't been working there very long when it became appar-ent that I was somehow making more than my boss. I wasn't just making a little more than he was; I was making several hundred dollars more. When he discovered this, he became furious. He would send me on wild goose chases, often to locate parts that should have been in stock but never seemed to be. It wasn't until some time later that I started to suspect this was his way of mak-ing things hard for me. He also colluded with his friends to make me look incompetent. He would work with the other directors to make sure I couldn't get a part we needed. When I reported to my supervisor that the parts were unavailable, he would curse at me, telling me to go and look for it again.

Shortly after I started, I met Nancy. She was a very attractive woman, about 5'6 with light, blonde hair, and a warm smile. She seemed to really enjoy my company, and she was always laughing at my jokes. I was still nervous about losing my job after having been unemployed, so I made sure to dress immaculately. Nancy took notice of this and often complimented me.

During my probationary period, I received a shock when my supervisor called me in and sat me down, saying I did not meet standards and would be terminated. I sat there in shock. I wondered if I hadn't I been polite enough to everyone? What could I have done differently? I mused.

As I spent my last few days saying good-bye while working, a couple who worked there—known as the Arnolds—called me into their office and explained to me the real reason I was being fired. They claimed my supervisor felt threatened. He hadn't gotten over the fact that I made more money than he did, but there was even more to it than that. Although he had been married for several years, he was in love with none other than Nancy.

"Are you serious?" I breathed.

"As a heart attack," said the husband solemnly. "He noticed she was flirting with you and started talking about having to let you go."

As I sat there, I started to grow angry. Here was proof that I was being setup once again. I envisioned myself storming into his office and confronting him. Suddenly, just like that, my anger left me. I got peace from realizing, Why would I fight to continue working under a man who was angry with me because of things out of my control? I could see now that he would never forgive me, neither for making more money than him nor for stealing the affection of the woman he wanted.

It was time for me to go. And so, once again, I found myself searching for a job. But this time, I decided to enlist the help of a job search company called Snelling and Snelling. They ended up sending me to Atlanta, Georgia, on April 7, 1969.

It was the day after my 26th birthday, and I was training to become an insurance agent. My job was to evaluate car insurance claims following accidents. I was the only black person in the entire class. I could almost feel the unease of my fellow classmates, especially the ones sitting closest to me. I did not feel like my instructor was particularly supportive of me. He always answered me in an aggressive tone, versus the friendly one he used when addressing the Caucasian students. He also liked to publicly berate me every chance he got. I couldn't stand it; it wasn't long before I was looking for a job once more.

Dejected, I saw no other options but to return to Tampa. The thought of returning to Tampa as a failure grieved me, but I could see no other way. That Saturday morning, I warmed up my 1969 lime green mustang and prepared to leave the hotel where I had been staying. As I said goodbye to some hotel staff I had grown to know, a young man whom I had befriended over the past few weeks informed me that next to the hotel was a federal agency, known as the Office of Economic Opportunity.

"If you stay over the weekend, maybe someone can help you," he suggested.

I thought about it and decided to wait to leave until after the weekend. What was the harm in talking to the federal agency? It's not like I had anything left to lose. So, I waited until Monday morning. As soon as the federal agency opened, I gave them a call. I was able to get in contact with a man named Marvin Stephens Arrington; I wouldn't find this out until later, but the man was something of a legend in Atlanta. He had played football at Morris Brown College and was very involved in the community; he would often participate in volunteer work, including speaking at events and educating others about the Civil Rights Movement. He was an attorney when I met him, but he would go on to become a Fulton County Commissioner, as well as a Fulton County Superior Court Judge.

When I met Marvin, I poured out all my troubles to him. I couldn't help it; I ended up telling him about my struggles after I graduated Bethune-Cookman College, and all the tribulations I had encountered in my jobs. I couldn't have been more surprised when he sympathized with me. Unbeknownst to me, Marvin always tried to help men get back on their feet, especially African American men; he considered it his calling from God. During that interview, he offered me $10,938 and asked me to consider working for him at the Office of Economic Opportunity.

"Of course, I accept!" I exclaimed. I was floored by this stranger's kindness.

"Great," Marvin said with a smile. "When can you start?"

"Yesterday," I joked.

I began working with him on June 23rd, 1969, and I would retire from the federal government 39 years later, on January 5, 2008.

It seemed like such a twisting road to get to where I needed to be. There were many days I was depressed or anger, unsure where I was going or what I should be doing. I felt like a failure, or a fool. But God always puts us right where we need to be. Unlike us, He can see the big picture. Whether you are a janitor or a CEO of a big company, He is always there to guide us to where we need to be, so we can become the person we are meant to be.

He was there all the time.

Chapter 13

THE SPIRIT OF FEAR

When I was living with Mama Dancil, she assigned me daily chores to do around the house. After completing my chores, I would go outside into the backyard. I liked to climb the many trees out there, whether it was one of the grapefruit trees or the mulberry trees. I would stay up in the branches for hours, picking any fruit that wasn't too ripe and eating it. I liked to watch the people go by, walking down the street and talking with one another. I liked the feeling of not being seen, of being hidden by the leaves. I watched the airplanes fly overheard, going to and from the Tampa Airport. I liked to imagine who was on those planes, and where they were going. I spent so many hours up in those trees that I started to dream of being in them. I remember a dream in which I was sitting in the huge oak tree in the front yard. Suddenly, I was caught up in a cloud of smoke and transported up to heaven.

Mama Dancil did not like worms of any kind. She was always

trying to rid the garden of them. I had no problem with them, as I liked all creatures, even the snakes I occasionally saw. But my feelings towards worms changed one day. I was playing in the backyard when I looked up and saw a web suspended in the persimmon tree. Curious, I took a long stick and prodded it. The stick went straight through the web and punched a hole into it. Suddenly, caterpillars poured out by the dozens. I barely managed to get out of the way before any landed on me. After that, I felt the same way about worms that Mama Dancil did. I still loved the other creatures in the backyard, even the snakes, but I could no longer stand worms.

Forty years later, I was living in Atlanta, Georgia. I was employed with the government, and I also taught Bible lessons at Ben Hill United Methodist Church. I would teach a different topic to my students every week. One week, the lesson was "Freedom from Fear." That night, I went home to my apartment, passing the several pecan trees that lined the property. Little did I know, there were dozens of caterpillar nests lining the trees. The following week, I was scheduled to travel out of state on business. In preparation for the trip, I decided to go to the Laundromat to wash some clothes. But when I looked outside my window, there were caterpillars everywhere. They were gathered on the roof of the house and spilling onto the front porch. In my mind, it seemed like they covered every inch of the yard. I summoned enough courage to run to my 1978 Cadillac Seville and, jumping over the worms to make it to the car.

At the Laundromat, I dreaded going home, as I knew what awaited me. I sat there, waiting for my clothes to dry and tried to figure out a way to avoid these little fuzzy, slow crawling creatures. Finding no logical way, I slowly drove home and sat in the car for a long time. As I had before, I summoned enough strength to jump over the worms that covered the driveway and porch. Once I got to the front door, I struggled holding the basket of clothes in one hand and trying to unlock the door with the other. The whole time, I felt like the worms were about to fall down the back of my shirt. Finally, I made it into the house, slamming the door shut behind me.

Once inside, I walked around the house summoning the courage to face my fears: the caterpillars. Later that night, as I was reading the Bible, I started to meditate on fear. I remembered what 2 Timothy 1:7 says about fear, stating, "God has not given us the spirit of fear, but of power, and of love and of a sound mind." I also recalled John 16:13, which tells us that the Spirit of truth will show you things to come. I had taught these scriptures for years, and I had just taught a lesson on fear to my students the previous week. Now, it was my turn to be tested.

Alright, Reginald, I thought to myself, it's time to practice what you preach. Focusing on the Word of God, I let its power resonate and settle within as I walked from room to room in the house. I kept saying to myself, "If you cannot practice it, don't preach it." Gathering strength from the scriptures I had read, I walked to the front door and opened it, peering outside and fully expecting to see an avalanche of caterpillars. But I saw nothing. Slowly, I opened the screen door and walked outside, stepping out onto the front yard and looking around. Still, there was nothing. I could not find even one worm.

Confused, I headed back into the house. I sat down, wondering what had happened. All of a sudden, the Spirit of God came to me and said, "When you dealt with your fear inside yourself, I dealt with the worms outside."

Initially, I thought His words meant that I had dealt with my fear while still inside my house. But then I realized that, although I was inside my house at the time, God really meant I had faced the fear that was inside my heart and soul. I remembered the words of 1 Peter 3:4, which says, "Rather, it should be that of your inner self, the unfading beauty of a gentle and quiet spirit, which is of great worth in God's sight."

Fear. There is no fear in God. Rather, it is part of our human nature to fear. It is something we are born with. Even though God tells us to not fear, and we try to listen, it is still something we feel on a regular basis.

I believe there is a time when we understand God's word, but do not yet know how to make His words a reality. I call this period the "Maturing Process". During this time, God will protect you from the things that you are afraid of, as you cannot yet do it yourself. He will guide us through the fears we experience, such as a mother lion guides her cubs through the wild. He will walk beside you, not allowing you to be faced with any fears that you cannot handle.

As you mature, you finally realize that you can live without fear of anything or anyone. Eventually, you get to the point of thinking about what a powerful life you could live if you never feared anything, including success or failure.

Is something like that possible? To live a life completely free of fear? Of course, it is. Study the life of Jesus. Try to see as Dr. Martin Luther King, Jr. did. When you find your purpose, and it is one worth dying for, you have no need to be afraid of any worldly thing. Each day, I am presented with my fears. Each day, I remember there is nothing to be afraid of, for I am reminded of the faithfulness and mercies of God. It is as 2 Corinthians 4:16 says, "Therefore we do not lose heart. Though outwardly we are wasting away, yet inwardly we are being renewed day by day."

He was there all the time.

YOUNG LOVE

I was in love with a girl named Loretta in elementary school, Although Loretta had no idea that I admired her, I would spend many hours daydreaming about us being together. One day, Loretta had to leave the school to go home early. I was watching her leave when I saw her handkerchief fall from her pocket and land onto the ground. I felt like it was fate as I rushed forward to retrieve it. I had seen things like this happen on T.V., and I just knew Loretta would fall madly in love with me when I handed her back her handkerchief. But when I snatched up her handkerchief and called out her name, she turned on me and said in an angry tone, "Give me back my handkerchief." I just stood there in shock as she snatched it from my hand.

Feeling dejected, I tucked my tail between my legs and headed back for my classroom. I felt like such a fool; the movies never showed the man getting his heart stomped out.

Loretta and I would go on to attend the same college and become great friends. We even laughed about the whole incident. After I moved to Atlanta, she came to visit me with her beautiful baby girl, Alexia. We remained friends until she joined the Lord in 2015.

.   .   .   .   .

You would think the handkerchief incident would be enough for me to stay away from girls, but no. Apparently, I needed more rejections. A few months passed after Loretta rejected me and I transferred to Carver Elementary School in West Tampa. This time, I had a crush on Patricia. Patricia was tall for her age, about 5'5, with dark skin and a sweet face. Just like with Loretta, I would see Patricia around school and imagine that we were together. One day, I was looking out of my classroom window when I saw her leaving campus. It was a hot, sunny day in Tampa and, although there was not a cloud in the sky, there was cloud of joy in my heart. I ran out to find Patricia, managing to catch up with her as she was crossing the baseball field. I called her name and she turned to look at me. For some reason, I was not fearful or apprehensive at all.

This is my opportunity to make a great first impression, I thought to myself. Wait until everyone sees me with Pat at lunch tomorrow!

I felt like we were already dating; I could already imagine my friends' reactions the next day after they found out I walked her home. I just knew that the two of us were about to become the talk of the school.

She was still looking at me, waiting for me to speak. I walked up to her and said gently, "Pat, can I walk you home?"

She looked at me as though I was a bug that had flown into her path.

"I wouldn't let you walk my spit home," she said, turning away to continue her walk home alone, as though I wasn't even there.

In no way was I prepared to hear those words come from such a sweet face. I was shocked. My head spun so fast and so hard that I felt like I might pass out.

As I stood there on that baseball field, I told myself she wasn't that great of a girl. I comforted myself by saying I didn't really like her anyway. Even after Pat and I became friends, I never allowed myself to like her in that way again. It was a long time before I was able to think about the incident without being mortified, but now I can look back on it and laugh.

In high school, I tried to get along with everyone. I took pride in my appearance and made sure to dress very well. I was also a bit quiet and shy. Despite this, I was very popular with the best athletes in the school. I still loved singing and, although I never officially joined the school choir, I sang during some of our assemblies.

There was a girl who I liked named Francis, whom I would talk to on occasion. One day, I noticed she wasn't eating anything at lunch. When I asked her why she wasn't eating, she said she didn't have any money. I didn't even hesitate; I just handed her my lunch money. I didn't mind going without for the day. I found out later that Francis gave the money to her boyfriend. I wasn't hurt, just embarrassed. One of my friends told me a lot of guys liked Francis, and she took things from them as well. Even though we had been duped, we all laughed about it.

The truth is, I have always loved girls. I think I inherited a lascivious spirit from my father. As a young man, my father did not drink, gamble or use drugs. He didn't have any vices except for one: he enjoyed the attention of women. I followed in his footsteps in this way; I never partook in any vices except for craving the attention of the opposite sex. As Exodus 20:5 tell us, "You shall not bow down to them or worship them; for I, the Lord our God, am a jealous God". Both my father and I were guilty of worshipping women and allowing them to replace Him in our hearts. It seemed I had inherited the sins of my father. But after receiving Jesus in my life, I vowed to break that generational curse. I was determined that our lascivious spirit would end in my generation.

I can still remember the day Mama Dancil asked me if I liked girls.

She had been teaching a piano class to two young ladies. I had been hovering in the dining room, which was next to the piano. After the girls left, Mama Dancil came up to me. She must have sensed something about me, even at that young age.

"Did you like those girls, Reginald?" she asked me.

"No ma'am," I replied.

I love them, I thought wickedly.

84

My grandmother was determined to not let me make the same mistakes my father did; she would often interrogate any young women who called the house looking for me, asking me if their families were respectable. Mama Dancil had a great deal of sense; I could not understand it at the time, but she was helping to direct my life towards purpose.

.   .   .   .

My wandering eye often got me in trouble, sometimes even putting my life at risk. There was one day where I was showing off for a lady at Pensacola Beach. I was vacationing there with Brunetta, the woman whom I was dating at the time. Brunetta was a very attractive woman with a curvy figure and long, dark hair. She was also highly intelligent and had many connections with several social and political figures in the Atlanta area.

While Brunetta lay sunning on the beach, I decided to swim farther into the ocean than anyone else. At one point, I heard her yell at me to not venture out so far. I took her words as a challenge; excited to have her attention, I swam out even further. It wasn't long before I realized there wasn't anyone around me. I looked back saw the shore far behind me. I had gone too far. I felt my panic start to rise. I turned around and began swimming back towards the shore, but for every stroke I made toward the shore a wave would take me back.

I was losing ground. I decided to use the waves coming from

shore to my advantage; when a wave came towards me, I would ride it back towards the shore. This worked for a while until I realized that I was being swept away from Brunetta and towards the pier.

Don't panic, I thought. Just pretend you're drifting toward the pier on purpose.

But as I continued to drift sideways, I realized that—due to the direction and rate I was travelling—I was liable to miss the pier altogether and end up drifting out to sea.

Even after realizing this, my pride would not let me call out for help. As Proverbs 16:18 says, "pride goes before the fall." My pride was about to cause me to drown. I started to panic as my arms grew more and more tired. There was no way I was going to make it back to shore. I called out to God, begging Him to help me. Isaiah 65:24 tells us, "before they call, I will answer, and while they are praying, I will hear". God heard me calling out to Him. It was only after I had surrendered my pride and asked for His help that He answered my prayers. As I kept using the waves to swim to shore, I suddenly felt sand under my feet. My body was shaking as I hurried back to the shore. I said a silent thanks to God, for He had delivered me from death once again.

Brunetta shook her head as soon as she saw me.

"You could have drowned," she said.

Now that I was back on shore, my pride came back in full force.

"I had things under control," I said, striving to sound like a macho man. But inside, I was still shaken. Brunetta had no idea how right she was.

As we drove back to Atlanta, I was still thanking God the entire way home.

He was there all the time.

Chapter 15

MY IDOLS

Two weeks before I graduated from college, I remember walking on campus and thinking how—now that I was 23-years-old—I was a man. And what was it that men wanted? Women.

Women, women and more women. That's truly what I believed. Because of that mentality, the next twelve years of my life would head steadily downhill.

From the time I was a little boy, I've always felt like I had a hole deep inside me. No matter what I tried to do to fill it, it remained empty. I tried to convince myself that I could fill it with the pleasure I got from sex, although it was fleeting and never filled it for very long.

I naturally have a quiet spirit; I believe God gave us two ears and one mouth for a reason. Because I was so good at listening, women would allow me access to their hearts and souls.

During college, I dated many kinds of women. There was a young lady, Barbara, I met while working for one of my college professors; we ended up dating for several months. She lived about two miles from campus, so I would have to leave the safety of the campus grounds to go see her. More often than not, I would be spotted by a group of white guys who randomly drove around town, most likely from boredom. They would chase me back onto campus, laughing and hurling racial slurs at me. One day, after this had happened and I'd returned to my dorm room, I looked into the mirror that hung over my desk and thought about how sick and tired I was. I was sick of going to Barbara's house and getting harassed by racist men in the process.

Why did I keep going over there, even knowing what was going to happen? For a few minutes of pleasure? Was that worth an hour of fear as I got chased around town? Was it worth the days of rage I felt afterwards?

"If anything keeps me out of heaven, it will be women," I said aloud, shaking my head.

A few years later, around 1970, I saved up enough to purchase a Mustang. It was a beautiful car, all lime green with a gold trim. One of my favorite things about it was the tag that sat on the front of the car; it was a picture of a wolf, with the words "Wolf Patrol" underneath. I was vain enough to think this tag represented how I was with women. I worked hard to seduce women; I made sure to dress immaculately and trim my hair regularly. Like any other naive male in their early 20's, I thought I was God's gift to women.

I had been told by a few of my older guy friends to think of women solely from the waist down. One of these so-called friends was the deacon at my church, who often brought his women over to my apartment for privacy. These men taught me to exercise what they called "The Three P's", which meant being polite, persistent and—above all—patient. Any man who possessed these characteristics was sure to get whatever he wanted from a woman. I was truly a wolf through those years; I had no discrimination towards women. I would try to sleep with a girl, then her sister and her best friend. In my quest to perfect the art of intimacy with a woman, I started to worship it as a god.

I remember a great aunt saying to me, "Reginald, a man chases a woman until she catches him." I didn't know what she meant until I met Sharon. She was a beautiful black woman who was very confident and flirtatious. I met her as she passed my apartment on her way to school. I was talking to several women at the time, but Sharon stood out from the others. She was a great conversationalist. We could talk for hours.

I have many great memories with Sharon, but not all our time together was happy. One night, when I was still teaching, she and I made a date for the evening. After work, I tried to call her to tell her I was on my way to her house. But the phone line was busy. I called several times, but the telephone stayed busy. When I arrived at her house, I knocked on the door but no one came to open it. I stood there for several minutes, knocking and calling out. Looking through the window next to the door, I could see Sharon sitting on her sofa and talking on the phone. I tried knocking again, but she didn't seem to hear me. Finally, my patience grew thin. I hit the window loud enough that she jumped up from the sofa; she abruptly hung up the phone and ran to the door to let me in.

"Where were you doing?" I asked her. "Why didn't you come to the door when I knocked?"

"I didn't hear you," she responded.

"Were you talking to someone?" I asked.

"No," she said, looking away.

"So, you weren't on the telephone?" I said slowly.

"No," she said again, still not looking at me.

I didn't know why Sharon was lying to me, but I had seen her on the phone with my own eyes.

"Sharon, look me in the eye and tell me you weren't on the phone," I said firmly.

She seemed hesitant, but she eventually did turn to face me.

"I was not on the phone," she said, looking me dead in the eye.

Despite this obvious lie, I continued to date her. While we were together, I was the happiest I had even been. She was not only beautiful, she was also smart. When I was with her, I never grew bored or tired. She was enough to keep me interested.

I decided to ask her to marry me. I was ready to hang up my title as womanizer. The wolf was ready to settle down, that is, until the day she broke my heart by calling off our engagement. It turns out she had been seeing another man behind my back.

I was a complete emotional wreck, as I thought everything had been going so well with us. I tried calling her and begging her to come back. She responded by mailing me back the engagement ring, along with a note asking me to never contact her or her family again. To top it all off, she signed the note with her new boyfriend's last name, as though they were already married.

Looking back, it's possible God sent her into my life as a type of punishment for my past actions with women. Up until that point in my life, I really had no consideration for a woman's feelings. I was polite, persistent and patient with them until I got what I wanted—then I was gone. You would think I would've seen this as a lesson from God and changed my ways. I didn't, though, and if anything, I became even more of a womanizer.

After the breakup, I cried for many nights. On one of those nights, I called out to the Lord, saying, "Lord, I have been told to never question you. But, I have to know... why me?" Even though I had sinned so many times in my life, even though I had wronged many women, I still asked God why this had to happen to me.

God knows what He is doing. He knew that bringing Sharon would be the best thing that could have ever happened to me. God knew that I needed to change my ways. I was no help to Him—or others—in the lustful state I had been. I needed someone to mirror the truth of my actions and how I had hurt others without a thought. Sharon did that for me.

I went into a depression. Even at work, my coworkers at the Department of Health and Human Services could tell I was not my usual self. One day, I sought advice from the office secretary, a kind, elder woman named Betty, who had experienced many of her own hardships in life. "Poor thing," she said to me. "At least it's all over except for the crying."

Another co-worker, Walter, told me only three things could help me: God, time, and other women. He told me to pray to God because prayer changes things, to give it time because it heals all things and spend an evening with another woman, so I could forget the first one. This was terrible advice especially for a person like me, as I took it as an excuse to return to my promiscuous ways.

For the next eight years, I drifted further and further away from God, as women became my idol once again. I was lucky to only catch an STD once, as I easily could've caught something that killed me. I ended up passing it onto one of the most decent women I have ever known, a beautiful thing named Belinda. Having to tell her to get checked was one of the lowest points of my life. I felt so ashamed in that moment, but it still wasn't enough to get me to change my ways.

Thankfully, I was never a gambler or a drinker. I had a few encounters with drugs, as did most people my age, but I never had much interest in them. I remember being introduced to marijuana by a guy named Jesse. He was living in the apartment adjacent to mine. One day, he asked me if I wanted to go on a ride with him. Having nothing better to do, I agreed. During the ride, he lit up a blunt and started blowing out smoke, which floated in the air all around me. I started to get lightheaded, and I was slow to respond to what he was saying to me. It took me a minute to realize I had a contact high. He pulled up to a street curb where two girls were standing in what had to be the shortest skirts I had ever seen. He started demanding money from them, which they handed over to him. That's when I realized Jesse was a pimp.

There was another time when a neighbor of mine invited me over. As I walked through his front door, I saw him bent over a tray. He pulled his head back to look at me, and I saw he had white powder all over his nose.

"Do you want some?" he asked, holding the tray out towards me.

Thank God for Mama Dancil, because it had to be her upbringing that made me say no.

Unfortunately, although I never got into drugs or drink, I was hopelessly addicted to women. More accurately, I was addicted to the physical pleasure I could get from them. I tried to sleep with almost every woman I came across. Some women even had boyfriends; whenever they had arguments with them, they would come over to my house. At the time, I thought I had it going on. These beautiful girls were with me when they had a man at home. It didn't occur to me until much later that they were using me just as much as I was using them.

During this time, I had a dream that I was riding on the bus. I knew I was on the way to work, and I was about to exit the bus when a beautiful woman got on the bus. I quickly sat back down. Not too long after that, I met a woman who bore a striking resemblance to the girl in my dream. She was a mild-mannered woman, quiet and approachable. As soon as our eyes met, the chemistry between us was apparent. Not only was she beautiful, she had a wonderful spirit and sweetness about her. Even though she was engaged to another man, we began sleeping together shortly after we met. She would often jokingly refer me to as forbidden fruit, since I was technically the "other man". One night, when she had stopped by my house to fool around, I stopped what I was doing and looked her in the eye.

"What do you know about God?" I asked suddenly.

"Really? You want to ask that at a time like this?" she said, surprised.

I don't know why I asked. It was like something came over me in that moment, and I wasn't truly myself. I knew her father was a preacher, and that made me think she would be interested in talking about God.

"Never mind," I said, rolling away from her.

Even though I had been brought up in church and knew God, the pursuit of sex took me away from Him. Somehow, over the years, I had replaced Him with something so fleeting as pleasure. I was like the Israelites when Moses left them, so concerned with having something to worship that I had made my own golden calf.

But despite all this, some part of me was still seeking Him out, even during my most intimate moments. It was like I knew what I truly craved was God's love, but I was unable to see or accept that until much later. He was always with me, no matter my sins. At the time, I just wanted to find a way to fill the emptiness inside me. I thought it was because of women that my heart was broken, when it was really from feeling absent from God. But even though I felt absent from Him, He never abandoned me. It is as Luke 4:18

tells us, "the Spirit of the Lord will heal the broken hearted." Even in my darkest moments, He was always there, guiding me.

He was there all the time.

Chapter 16

THE BEGINNING OF WISDOM

A good friend of mine, the late Archbishop Earl Paulk, mentioned a term that has always stayed with me. It was a term I had never heard before, but it described a principle I had always believed to be true. The term is "transubstantiation." Transubstantiation is defined as though the appearance of the elements of the Lord's Supper bread and wine remain the same. They are transformed into the actual body and blood of Jesus. They do not represent his body and blood; they are his body and blood.

One day, while I was at home preparing to deliver a message at a friend's church, I began to truly study the term. I wondered why the church placed so much emphasis on the body and blood of Jesus, and not something else. Why not the breath of Jesus, for instance? I pulled out my chalkboard along with a cup used from a past communion and a piece of bread. As I pondered the items, I had an open vision. I felt the presence of God enter the room, hovering over the bread and cup. Sensing Him so close to me, I began to weep. I felt like He had appeared to show me the truth of transubstantiation.

I had sent another open vision, in which I saw Jesus walking the street and carrying the cross. There were people on either side of Him, jeering and calling out insults. My heart broke at the sight. Here was our savior, our Lord. As He walked, bent under the weight of the cross, He looked straight at me and said, "I'm doing it for you." Needless to say, my life has never been the same. No matter my sins, God has never abandoned me.

A pivotal point in my life was Pastor Kirby Clements laying his hands on me in prayer. At the time, there were a lot of women looking on, and I was embarassed to receive prayer. The spirit of God spoke to me and said, "If you are ashamed of me before man, then I will be ashamed of before my Father." I immediately let him pray for me, and my life has never been the same.

Throughout my life, I have had to recall this vision and call on scriptural wisdom to get me through the incidents I have described in the previous chapters, as well as though I have may have overlooked or may have inadvertently determined to be insig-nificant. Nevertheless, these are the passages that have anchored me then and still now.

1) St. John 3:3: "Jesus replied, "Very truly I tell you, no one can see the kingdom of God unless they are born again." Every person is born into sin. Being born again is the changing of your nature.

2) 1 Corinthians 6:9 says, "or do you not know that wrongdoers will not inherit the kingdom of God? Do not be deceived: Neither the sexually immoral nor idolaters nor adulterers nor men who have sex with men." Fornicators have no inheritance in the kingdom of God.

3) Colossians 1:16 tells us, "For in him all things were created: things in heaven and on earth, visible and invisible, whether thrones or powers or rulers or authorities; all things have been created through him and for him." We were all created by God and for God.

4) Isaiah 43:7 says, "Everyone who is called by my name, whom I created for my glory, whom I formed and made." We were created for God's glory. Live in purpose. Purpose is found in the gifts and natural abilities that God has granted us. God endows every person with the gifts necessary to fulfill God's purpose.

5) Philippians 2:13 tells us, "13 For it is God who works in you to will and to act in order to fulfill his good purpose." Yield to His will, for God will lead and guide you in understanding your heavenly and earthly purpose.

6) Deuteronomy 8:18 says, "But remember the LORD your God, for it is he who gives you the ability to produce wealth, and

so confirms his covenant, which he swore to your ancestors, as it is today." The Lord God gives power to get wealth.